I was Kissed
by a Seal
at the Zoo

I was Kissed by a Seal at the Zoo

BOOK CLUB EDITION

BEGINNER BOOKS

A DIVISION OF RANDOM HOUSE, INC.

BY HELEN PALMER
with photographs by
LYNN FAYMAN

What would you do
if you went to the zoo?

Well, I can tell you what I would do.
I would walk right up
to the lion keeper.
I would say, "Please,
may I play with your baby lion?"

"Yes," he would say,
"if the lion wants to play."

5

Then I would walk
right up to the lion.
"Lion," I would say,
"will you play ball
with me?"

"That is not a ball!
That is my hanky!
Now come on down here.
I will show you how to play."

Then I would say,
"Take a look
at this ball.
You see it?"

8

"First I will throw it.
Then you try to catch it."

"You did it!
You did catch it!
Good for you!"

Then I would say, "Thank you.
I had fun with your lion."

That is what I would do
if I went to the zoo.
Now what would you do?

If I went to the zoo, I would
make friends with a walrus.
First I would give him some water.

Then I would put my hand
on his head.
"Walrus," I would say,
"I am your friend.
I am going to do
something for you—
something that no one
has ever done before."

"I am going to read to you."
Then I would read
a funny book to him.

I know he would like it.
I would like it
if I were a walrus.

If I went to the zoo
I would take my little brother.
I would take him for a walk
under the tall trees.
I would show him
how pretty the zoo is.
I would show him
how big the zoo is.
I would show him all of it!

I would show him a goat,
a little white goat.

Then I would feed
the little white goat.

But if something big
came around,
I would get out of there fast.

My brother and I
like little animals.

If I went to the zoo,
I would play with something big.
Big turtles!

I would tell those big turtles
what to do.
I would be a traffic cop.

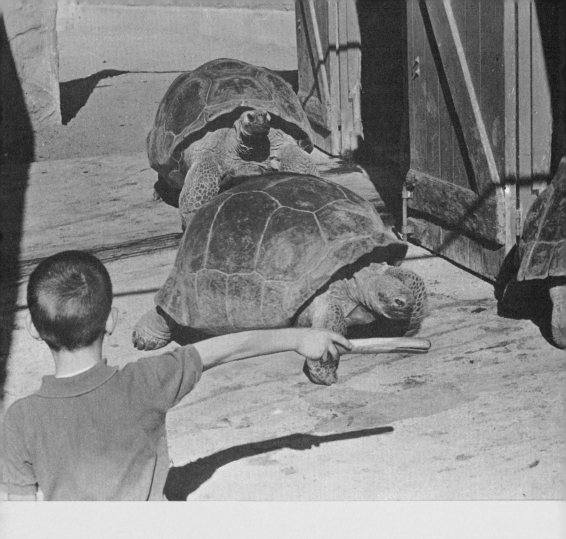

I would say,

"Come on, now!

Hurry up!

Get along there!"

Then I would hop on
the biggest one of all!
He would take me for a ride.

If I went to the zoo,
I would help the elephant keeper.

I would help put
the baby elephant in his pen.
I would give him a push—
a hard push.

Maybe I would push too hard.
Maybe that baby elephant
would fall down!

So I would help him up.
And I would get him
into his pen.

Then the keeper
would call to some one.
"Milk! Bring some milk
for our little elephant!"

I would help him
drink the milk.
Every one in the zoo
would come around and say,
"Look at that boy feed
that elephant!"

I like the funny ones.
If I went to the zoo,
I would find one
with lots of humps and bumps.

I would say, "Hello, Hump-Bump.
Here! Have a cookie."
And that funny old camel
would eat it. Glump! Glump!

I like the pretty ones.
The zoo is full of them.
Some of them
will let you pet them.
I would pet a gazelle.

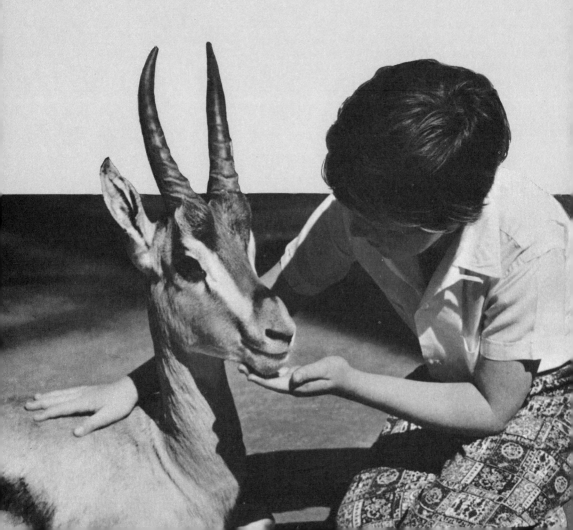

Then I would look around
and find a sheep to pet.
He would let me hold
his head in my hands.

What would I do
if I went to the zoo?

Well, I know a chimp there.
This chimp loves grapes.
This chimp will eat grapes
all day, if you let him.
So I would give him
MILLIONS of grapes,
one after another.

I would play a game
with that chimp.
He likes to play
a very funny game—
the shoe game.

He takes off your shoes.
Then you put them back on.
He will play the shoe game
all day, if you let him.

What would I do?

Well, I know that chimp.

I know he likes trains.

I would take him on a train ride.
That chimp will ride
all day, if you let him!

I know that chimp, too.
But I know what
he likes best of all.
He likes you to
pick him up and hold him.
That chimp will
hold on to you all day,
if you let him.
And I know I will let him.

If I went to the zoo

I would go to the Bear Tree.

I love those big black bears.

I would like to go

right in there with them.

I would like to go

right up their tree.

But no one can go in with bears.

SO . . .

45

I would go in with the penguins.

I think the keeper would let me do that.

I like penguins.

Penguins look like little men,
little men in black and white coats.
I would make them get in line.

Maybe some penguin would not want
to get in line. Then I would say,
"Come here, Mr. Penguin!
Do as you are told."

Then I would walk up
to that line of little men.
And I would give
every one of them a fish.

Do you know what I
would do at the zoo?

I would go to the seal show.
I would see the seals do tricks.

After the show

I would say to the trainer,

"I like this seal.

Is he tired?

Is he too tired to play with me?"

The trainer would say,

"I don't know.

Why don't you ask him?"

"Well," I would ask,
"how about it, old boy?
Do we play?
Or don't we play?"

Then he would tell me in seal talk,
"O.K.   O.K."

Then what a ball game
we would have!

And how that seal
would like it!

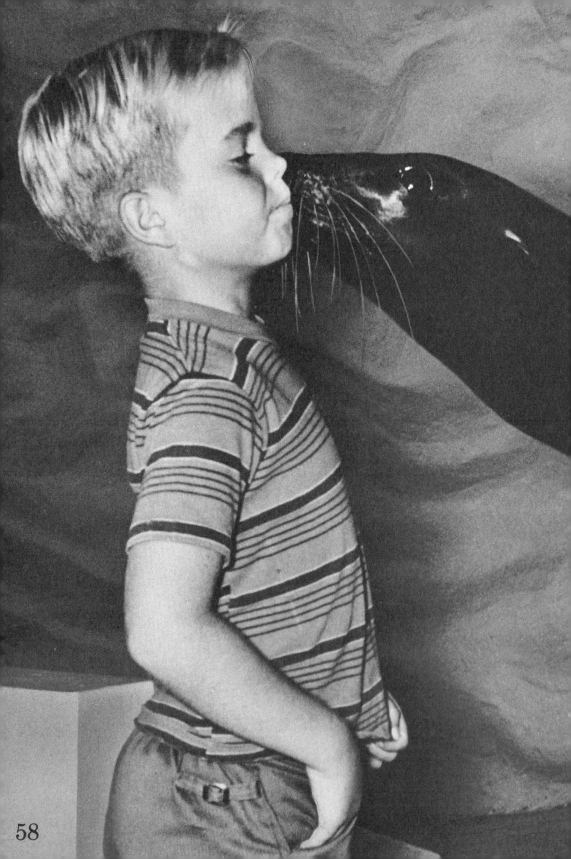

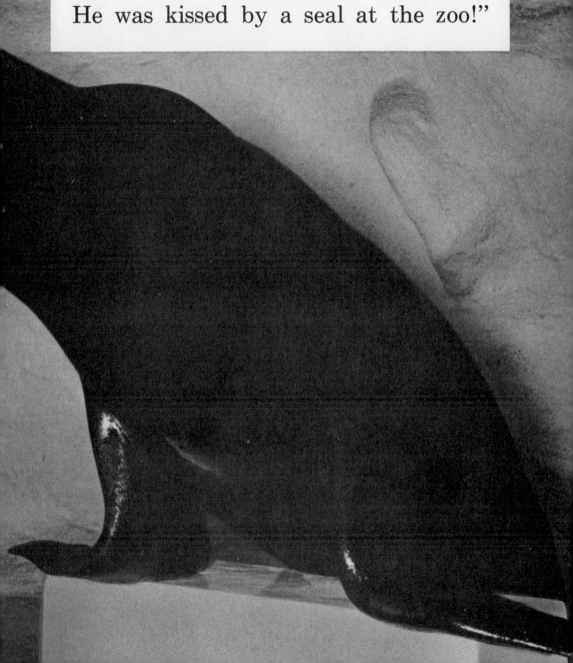

That seal would like it so much
he would kiss me.
Then every one would say, "That boy!
He was kissed by a seal at the zoo!"

Those are the things
we would do at the zoo.
And do you know something?
We went there!
And we did them.

We are mostly kids
from the Francis Parker School
in San Diego, California.
We want to thank the Zoo Director,
Dr. C. R. Schroeder, and all the men
and all the women and all the animals
for all the fun they gave us
at the San Diego Zoo.